Baltimore Orioles
A Science I CAN READ Book
by Barbara Brenner

Pictures by J. Winslow Higginbottom

Harper & Row, Publishers
New York, Evanston, San Francisco, London

For Evan

Library of Congress Catalog Card Number: 73–14327
Trade Standard Book Number: 06–020664–0
Harpercrest Standard Book Number: 06–020665–9
FIRST EDITION

Contents

1. They Come

It is a day in May.

Apple trees are in bloom.

The yard is warm with sun.

Suddenly something flies by.

Bright orange and black.

A bird.

It is the male Baltimore oriole.

He flies to an apple tree

in front of the house.

Then he flies to the yard.

He lands in a maple tree.

He calls and sings from there.

He is telling other birds

to keep away.

Three days later she comes.

The female.

Pale orange and olive-green.

She flies to the maple tree.

The male is waiting for her.

He sings sweetly to her.

He bows.

He bobs up and down.

His colors flash at her.

Orange, black, white.

Orange, black, white.

She watches him

show off his colors.

She sings to him.

The people in the house

hear the orioles singing.

12

Now the two birds stay together.

They fly around the yard.

They call back and forth.

They feed each other caterpillars.

They mate.

Soon they will nest

and have baby birds.

2. Nesting

The orioles choose a branch
high in the maple tree.
Here the female begins
to make a nest.

16

She finds soft grasses

and dry plants

and bits of string.

She weaves them together

with her beak.

She shapes the nest
with her feet and her body.
Sometimes she hangs upside down
as she works.

Her mate stays near her.

He watches, and sings

his "keep-away" song.

One, two, three, four, five days.

The nest is done.

There it hangs,

a soft, gray bag.

Deep, and strong,

and safe.

The people in the house

do not know the nest is there.

3. Hatching

Now the female lays

an egg in the nest.

The next day she lays another egg.

And the next day.

And the next.

One egg each day.

Four eggs.

They are much smaller than hens' eggs.

They are white

with brown spots and lines.

Inside each egg

a baby oriole is growing.

If the eggs are kept warm

they will hatch.

23

The mother bird
stays in the nest.

She sits on the eggs.

Some of her feathers fall out.

Her bare skin is
right over the eggs.

Her skin is warm.

It keeps the eggs warm.

The father bird

stays near his mate.

He watches out for danger.

One day danger comes.

Danger has a bushy tail.

It is a red squirrel.

Red squirrels eat birds' eggs.

The orioles see the squirrel.

The female calls out loudly.

The male flies at the squirrel

and pecks it with his beak.

The squirrel runs away.

Mother goes back to her eggs.

Father goes back to his branch.

Danger has gone.

4. Baby Birds

One morning there are sounds
inside the eggs.
Hatching sounds.
Four baby birds peck their way
out of the eggshells.

30

They have no feathers.

Their heads are big.

Their necks are skinny.

Their eyes are closed.

31

But their mouths are open.

They are hungry.

Mother feeds them.

First she finds a bug or worm.

She swallows it.

She flies back to the nest.

She spits up the food

into the mouths of her babies.

Now Father takes a turn.

Up. Down.

Up. Down.

The orioles feed their babies

all day long.

The babies eat

and sleep

and grow.

In a week they have feathers.

They all look like their mother—
pale orange and olive-green.
Later the male babies will be
bright orange like their father.
The babies begin to make sounds.
"Teedee! Teedee! Teedee!"
Father and Mother feed them
when they make that sound.
Now they feed them whole food.
Ants. Spiders. Caterpillars.
The babies are growing up.

5. Young Birds

One day Father Bird

sees a new danger.

A big, black bird.

A crow.

Crows eat baby birds.

Father flies at the crow.

But the crow is so big!

And it moves so fast!

It grabs a baby bird and flies away.

The mother bird

calls her lost baby

until it is dark.

But the baby is gone.

She has only three babies now.

Another week passes.

The three young orioles

come out of the nest.

They hang on to its side.

They cannot fly yet.

It is a long way to the ground.

They may slip and fall.

Mother must get them down.

She stops feeding them.

They are hungry.

They call for food.

Mother flies down

to a lower branch

of the maple tree.

She calls them.

She has a caterpillar

in her mouth.

The young birds see it.

They hop down to the lower branch

to get it.

She gives it to them.

Now she flies lower.

She calls them again.

She has some bugs in her mouth.

They see the bugs.

They hop down to get them.

She feeds them each a bug.

This way, the mother oriole

leads her young ones down.

She leads them into a bush.

They will hide in its branches

until they can fly.

6. Hiding

There is danger

near the ground too.

It comes on quiet paws.

Father Bird does not hear it.

Mother Bird does not see it.

It pounces!

A young bird cries out,

"Teedee! Teedee! Teedee!"

Mother and Father Bird fly

to a nearby tree.

But they are afraid to come down.

The people in the house

hear the young bird's cry.

They run into the yard.

"Bad cat!" they say.

"Drop it!"

The cat drops the bird.

Poor little oriole.

Its eyes are closed.

Is it dead?

No. Its heart is beating.

The little oriole opens its eyes.

The people bring it

into the house.

They know orioles like cherries.

They give the young oriole

a piece of cherry.

It eats.

They give it another piece.

It eats that too.

It eats the whole cherry.

Now the people know

the little oriole

will be all right.

They bring it back to the yard.

It begins to call "Teedee!"

The mother bird hears.

She swoops down.

She calls.

The little oriole

flops onto the grass.

It hops toward its mother.

She calls to it again.

The little bird runs under the bush.

It hides in the leaves

with the other young orioles.

7. They Come and Go

Soon the birds are old enough to fly.

One, two, three young orioles

leave the yard.

Mother and Father leave too.

They all fly into the woods.

But they do not stay together.

In July the yard is quiet.
In August the male comes
to the yard alone.
The people hear his song.

In September, Baltimore orioles
leave the woods and trees.
They fly south.

Winter comes.

The maple tree is bare.

Now the people in the house

can see the oriole nest.

And then—

it is spring again.

A day in May.

Apple trees are in bloom.

The yard is warm with sun.

Suddenly something flies by.

Bright orange and black.

It is a male Baltimore oriole.

The same one.

He has come back to nest

in the same maple tree.

Three days later she comes.

A female.

The male is waiting for her. . . .

AUTHOR'S NOTE

The Baltimore oriole is an American bird. The first set-
tlers had never seen a bird quite like it. They called it
"Hang-nest" and "Firebird" and "Golden bird." Later
they named it "Baltimore bird" because its colors were
like the family colors of the Lords of Baltimore. The
oriole part came from a Latin word which means *golden*.
There are twenty-eight species of birds in the family of
Orioles, but the Baltimore oriole is not a true oriole. It
belongs to the family *Icteridae*.

In the old days Baltimore orioles made their nests out
of horsehair. The nests were almost always in elm trees.
When cars began to take the place of horses, and elm trees
began to disappear, the Baltimore oriole had to change its
ways. Now it nests in maples and oaks and even in birch
trees. It uses grass and plant stems to make its nest. But it
still weaves the same hanging bag it made long ago. And it
has a habit of coming back to the same place every year.